The Life And Death Of St. Pancras, A Young Martyr [&c.]

THE

LIFE AND DEATH

OF

ST. PANCRAS,

A

YOUNG MARTYR

OF

THE EARLY CHRISTIAN CHURCH.

London:

WILLIAM POOLE, 12A, PATERNOSTER ROW.

THE

LIFE AND DEATH

OF

ST. PANCRAS,

A

YOUNG MARTYR

OF

THE EARLY CHRISTIAN CHURCH,

WHO WAS SLAIN AT ROME IN THE REIGN OF THE
EMPEROR DIOCLETIAN,

A.D. 304.

WITH NOTES AND APPENDIX,

CONTAINING A LETTER TO THE YOUNG ON PERSECUTION,
AND THOUGHTS ON THE COMMEMORATION
OF DEPARTED FRIENDS.

———◆———

𝕷𝔬𝔫𝔡𝔬𝔫 :

WILLIAM POOLE, 12A, PATERNOSTER ROW.

Fight the good fight of faith.—1 Tim. vi.

I, even I, am He that comforteth you. Who art thou, that thou shouldest be afraid of a man that shall die, and of the son of man, which shall be as grass; and forgettest the LORD thy Maker?—Isaiah li.

The Lord is my light and my salvation; whom, then, shall I fear? The Lord is the strength of my life; of whom then shall I be afraid?—Psalm xxvii.

The Son of God goes forth to war,
 A kingly crown to gain,
His blood-red banner streams afar!
 Who follows in His train?
Who best can drink his cup of woe,
 Triumphant over pain,
Who patient bears his cross below,
 He follows in His train.

The martyr first, whose eagle eye
 Could pierce beyond the grave,
Who saw his Master in the sky,
 And called on him to save.
Like Him, with pardon on His tongue
 In midst of mortal pain,
He prayed for them that did the wrong;
 Who follows in His train?

A glorious band, the chosen few
 On whom the Spirit came,
Twelve valiant saints, their hope they knew,
 And mocked the cross and flame.
They met the tyrant's brandished steel,
 The lion's gory mane,
They bowed their necks, the death to feel;
 Who follows in their train?

A noble army, men and boys,
 The matron and the maid,
Around the Saviour's throne rejoice,
 In robes of white arrayed.
They climbed the steep ascent of heaven,
 Through peril, toil, and pain;
O God, to us may grace be given
 To follow in their train. Amen.

CONTENTS.

~~~~~~~

The Life and Martyrdom of St. Pancras .. .. 5—11

Persecution in the Reign of Diocletian 12

The Martyrdom of St. Alban 13

The Strength of the Martyrs .. .. .. ib.

Youthful Martyrs 18

Saying "Yes" to Jesus 19

Persecution.—A Letter to the Young 22

Commemoration of Departed Friends 39

Shall we Meet? 43

The Meeting-Place 45

Prayers 46

"HE, BEING MADE PERFECT IN A SHORT TIME, FULFILLED A LONG TIME: FOR HIS SOUL PLEASED THE LORD; THEREFORE HASTED HE TO TAKE HIM AWAY FROM AMONG THE WICKED."

THE LIFE AND MARTYRDOM

OF ST. PANCRAS.

Some of my readers may have pictured to themselves St. Pancras as a venerable old man, like Polycarp or Ignatius. If so, they are quite mistaken. Pancratius (for that was his Latin name) was a boy about fifteen years of age when he suffered martyrdom.

He was the son of an ancient and wealthy Roman nobleman, and was born in Phrygia*, and spent the first ten years of his life at Synnada. His mother, of whom he was devotedly fond, had brought him up with tender care; and his childish days were very happy. When only nine years of age he lost this beloved parent; and Cleonius, his father, buried her beside the waters of a brook which flowed through their estate. Every day, for three months, did he and his little boy Pancras visit the mother's grave, to weep

---

* Phyrgia was visited by St. Paul when he confirmed the Churches in Galatia.

over and strew flowers upon the soil under which she rested.

If they had known of JESUS and the Resurrection, those flowers might have reminded them of a life of happiness and glory above the grave. But at that time the mind of Pancratius was in heathen darkness. He was soon to be enlightened with the blessed hope of immortality which is the inheritance of every true Christian.

At the end of three months Cleonius died of grief for the loss of his wife. On his death-bed he called for his brother, and earnestly entreated him to take charge of his little boy Pancras, and educate him as though he were his own son.

The boy's uncle promised faithfully to carry out the request of his dying brother. He thought that the best way to fulfil that wish would be to take Pancratius to Rome (then the greatest city of the greatest empire in the world), that there he might have the advantage of superior instruction, and when he grew older he would perhaps obtain a good position in the State.

ROME.

IT was in the reign of the Emperor Diocletian, about the year of our Lord 304, that the youth and his uncle found themselves in

Rome. The Christian religion was then bitterly persecuted, and many of the disciples of our Lord had sealed their testimony with their blood. At that time there lived among the Christians at Rome a pastor, or bishop of the church, whose name was Marcellinus. This devoted man was in the habit of going secretly from house to house, affectionately telling the heathen Romans whom he could get to listen to him, that JESUS, the despised Nazarene, was the Saviour of mankind.

The Emperor Diocletian was a bitter enemy to the Christians; and among those men who assisted him in his persecutions was his minister, Galerius, a man even more cruel than himself, and who at last persuaded him to put all the Christians to death. In consequence of this cruel resolve, proceedings were at once taken, and many professing the new religion were put to excruciating deaths; some being flayed alive, and others thrown to the wild beasts.

Marcellinus expected from day to day that his own turn would come, and he went from house to house, at the dead of night, when heathen Rome was slumbering, to cheer the desponding, and to confirm the faith of the wavering.

CONVERSION.

ONE night, as Marcellinus was engaged in this good and courageous work, guided by the good providence and the Spirit of God, he entered the house in which resided the young Pancratius and his uncle. He earnestly explained to them the doctrines of the new faith. They listened and believed. They gradually forsook the worship of the temple of Jupiter, and often at midnight, with lighted torches in their hands, they would go to the catacombs * of Rome, there to meet with Christian friends, and celebrate with them the Lord's Supper. At the approach of morning they returned to their homes, invigorated and strengthened against the terrors of death, and resolved to confess Christ before all men.

The portion of Scripture which Marcellinus often read and expounded was the Gospel of St. John, and the orphan boy and his uncle repeated to each other all they could remember of what they heard in the catacomb. The uncle, however, died soon after his conversion, leaving young Pancras alone in the world, and almost broken-hearted.

---

* The Catacombs are vast caverns beneath the City of Rome, used in ancient times by Christians for the burial of the dead.

HE CONFESSES CHRIST BEFORE THE EMPEROR.

ONE day, when kneeling beside the body of of his uncle in earnest prayer, four Roman soldiers entered the room, and one of them, laying his hand upon the youth's shoulder, bade him rise and prepare to enter the presence of the Emperor. Brushing away his blinding tears, Pancratius rose from his knees; a chain was fastened to his wrists, and after taking a last fond gaze at the calm features of his dead uncle, he followed the guard to the imperial palace of the Cæsars.

It is said that though his young arms ached with the heavy chains, and his feet were blistered with his fast walk, he displayed a remarkably pleasant and cheerful countenance during his journey along the streets of Rome. Being the son of a nobleman, there is no doubt he was considered worthy of a trial. The Emperor Diocletian was seated on his throne, surrounded by all the *insignia* of royalty and power, when the weak footsore child was led into the monarch's presence: and a very striking spectacle it must have appeared, to see a feeble youth, conscious of the strength of his faith in Christ, thus braving with undaunted courage the majesty of imperial Rome. The Em-

peror himself, bitter as he was against the
Nazarenes, was moved with pity when he
saw the youthfulness of the convert whom he
had ordered to be brought before him. Instead of using threats, he tried to win him
over by promises. He reminded the boy of
his father and mother, how in their dying
days they had been faithful to the gods of
their ancestors, and he promised to take him
under his protection, and eventually place
him in a high position, if he would only offer
a sacrifice to Jupiter. But the child steadfastly refused. The Emperor then turned
to threats; he told him that he should be
killed that very day ; that he should not live
an hour longer, and that his body should be
thrown to the wild beasts. It is recorded
that pale and trembling, he boldly answered :
"THAT MAY BE, BUT I DARE NOT DENY MY
SAVIOUR, I DARE NOT WORSHIP IDOLS.
GOD WILL GIVE ME STRENGTH TO DIE FOR
HIM AS OTHERS HAVE DONE."

"Lead the obstinate boy from my presence," exclaimed the infuriated Diocletian;
"take him to the Aurelian Way, and de-
spatch him with your swords."

MARTYRDOM.

THE same legionaries who had brought him
to the palace led him out to the place where

the Monarch had directed. It was sunset. And kneeling down, with his hands tied behind him, the noble boy died, pierced by the swords of his persecutors. Late in the evening some kind Christian ladies went to the place of his martyrdom, brought away his mangled corpse, and buried it in the catacombs of Rome.

For many years after this Pancratius was forgotten. But on the conversion of the Emperor Constantine, his bones were removed to a sacred spot, and a magnificent church was erected over his burial-place. From this Church at Rome the old and new churches of St. Pancras, in London, have derived their name *.

* * * * *

Another account states that Pancratius was thrown to the lions.

Two scenes in the life of St. Pancras are represented on the beautiful bridge which crosses the Regent's Canal near Gloucester Gate, Regent's Park.

1. Bishop Marcellinus giving his blessing to Pancratius.

2. Pancratius attacked and slain by a lion.

---

* It is said of the Church of St. John Lateran at Rome : " This is the head and Mother of all Christian churches, if you except that of St. Pancras, under High-gate, near London." The common seal of St. Pancras parish represents a youthful saint trampling upon heathen superstition. There are seven churches dedicated to St. Pancras in England, and many others in Italy and France.

THE PERSECUTION IN THE REIGN
OF DIOCLETIAN.

THE Tenth Persecution of the Christian Church, in the reign of Diocletian, lasted nineteen years, and was the most heart-rending and bloody on record. Imperial proclamations were set up everywhere, forbidding the assembling together of the Christians for divine worship; churches were demolished and overthrown to their foundations; the Holy Scriptures were burnt; Christians who enjoyed any honours were deprived of them; rich men were deprived of their liberty if they persisted in the profession of Christianity. Such was the first proclamation. Soon after, by other edicts, it was ordered that all presidents of churches should be cast into prison, and then, by all ways imaginable, compelled to offer sacrifice to the false gods of Rome.

The prisons were filled with Christians, and there appeared a third proclamation, in which it was ordained that they who were in prison should be set at liberty if they would offer sacrifice; but that they who refused should be subjected to all kinds of torments.

Immediately on the appearance of these commands, Eusebius informs us that he saw "houses of prayer demolished to the foundation, and the divinely-inspired and sacred Scriptures burnt in the market-places;" and he also gives us an account of the vast numbers that were imprisoned, racked, tortured, and put to death in the cause of Christ. Many, weak in the faith, in order to save themselves, too readily gave up their copies of the sacred Scriptures; whence they ever after acquired the name of *Traditores* *.

---

* Eusebius. Ecclesiastical History, VIII.

THE MARTYRDOM OF ST. ALBAN.

AT this period also fell the first British martyr, *St. Alban ;*
who, having concealed a preacher named Amphibalus,
was brought before the governor, and there confessing
himself a Christian, he was immediately ordered to the
torture, and soon after beheaded near the town of Verulam
(St. Alban's), his native place. A church was built upon
this spot, and dedicated to St. Alban. It was afterwards
enlarged, and is now known as St. Alban's Abbey.

O ALMIGHTY God, we most humbly praise Thy glorious
name for Thy grace given to Thy servants, who have
departed this life in Thy faith and fear, and for Thy
countless blessings shed forth upon Thy people everywhere : Grant unto us, we beseech Thee, that being
compassed about with so great a cloud of witnesses, we
may run with patience the race that is set before us, and
with them attain to the resurrection of the just ; through
Jesus Christ our Lord. Amen.

THE STRENGTH OF THE MARTYRS.

WHY did Daniel and his friends stand firm at Babylon ?
Why did they choose a cruel and painful death rather
than a life of luxury and splendour ? Why did Daniel
kneel in prayer three times a day ? Why was he pre-
served from the death which he feared ? "Because he
believed" in the God of his fathers.—Dan. vi.

Why did the Christian martyrs submit to all the bar-
barities which the Roman tyrants could invent ? Why
did they labour as bondsmen, maimed and miserable, in
dark underground caverns ? Because they trusted and
loved their Lord and Saviour, Jesus Christ. They
believed in the Christ of St. Paul, and therefore they
could say, in all the sincerity and power of a living faith,
"*None of these terrors move me. I know whom I have
believed.*"

A word, a sign, of submission to the pagan religion

would have restored them to liberty, and saved them from a painful death. But that word they would not utter : that sign they refused to give. They knew that life purchased upon such terms would not be worth having. They believed that the Son of God had saved them from the wrath to come, and that He had passed through sufferings unknown to man, to open the Kingdom of Heaven to all believers. In the hour of trial and temptation they were sustained by the presence of a merciful Saviour, and by the prospect of an immortal crown.

They dreaded the sword, and the fire, and the fury of savage beasts ; they felt keenly the rage and mockery of their powerful enemies. But the fear and love of God prevailed over all these terrors. How could they forget Christ's words?—"*Fear not them which kill the body, but are not able to kill the soul: but rather fear Him who is able to destroy both soul and body in hell.*"—St. Matthew x. ; St. Luke x.

"*Fear not, little flock; for it is your Father's good pleasure to give you the Kingdom.*"—St. Luke x.

"*Whosoever, therefore, shall confess Me before men, him will I confess also before My Father Who is in heaven. But whosoever shall deny Me before men, him will I also deny before My Father Who is in heaven.*"—St. Matt. x.

Lord of heaven and earth, teach us to fear Thee, the Almighty and all-seeing God; help us to trust in Thee as our merciful Father ; and, supported by the remembrance of Thy presence, and by the hope of Thy protection, let us not fear what man may say or do unto us, as long as we obey Thy holy will. Amen.

"Wherefore seeing we also are compassed about with so great a cloud of witnesses, let us lay aside every weight, and the sin which doth so easily beset us, and let us run with patience the race that is set before us. Looking unto Jesus, the author and finisher of our faith ; who for the joy that was set before him endured the cross, despising the shame, and is set down at the right hand of the throne of God."—Hebrews xii.

Grant, O Lord, that I may bear all the troubles of this life with a meek and patient spirit, without repining at what Thou shalt appoint for the discipline of my soul. I will look unto Thee, O Jesus, when Thou wast in the place of sinners, with what patience Thou didst bear the scorn, the anger, the unrighteous judgment, the miserable death of the cross. And this, by Thy grace, shall be my pattern. Amen.

"Whosoever shall confess Me before men, him will I confess also before my Father Who is in Heaven."—St. Matthew x.

O Lord Jesu Christ, for Whose coming to Judgment Thy Church is waiting, come now to us in Thy quickening love, and so plant Thy holy fear and love in our hearts, and endue us with such boldness to confess Thee before men, that Thou mayest confess us before Thy Father and all the angels in heaven, that, together with all Thy faithful servants, we may inherit the kingdom prepared for us before the foundation of the world, through Thy merits and mediation, to whom be all praise and honour for ever. Amen.

"Be thou faithful unto death, and I will give Thee a crown of life."—Rev. ii.

O my Saviour! how long have I professed to follow Thee without following the blessed steps of Thy most holy life! Help me to remember Thy *patience* and *humility*, Thy great disregard for the world, its pleasures, profits, honours, and all its idols; Thy merciful concern for the miseries of men, Thy unweariedness in doing good, Thy constancy in prayer, and resignation to the will of Thy Father. Let me part with anything as dear as a right hand or a right eye, rather than not follow Thee. O Lord, obtain for me the spirit of self-denial, that I may follow Thee, as I hope to live with Thee for ever. Amen.

I reckon that the sufferings of this present time are not worthy to be compared with the glory which shall be revealed in us."— Romans viii.

GRANT, O Lord, that, in all our sufferings here upon

earth, for the testimony of Thy truth, we may steadfastly look up to heaven, and by faith behold the glory that shall be revealed ; and, being filled with the Holy Ghost, may learn to love and bless our persecutors by the example of Thy first martyr Saint Stephen, who prayed for his murderers to Thee, O blessed Jesus, who standest at the right hand of God to succour all those that suffer for Thee, our only Mediator and Advocate. Amen.

"Grant, O Lord, that in all our sufferings here upon earth for the testimony of Thy truth, we may steadfastly look up to heaven." These words are no dead letter, even in an age and country where direct persecution for religious opinions has passed away. The example of true Christians, quietly and consistently upheld, cannot but arouse the enmity of some portion of "*the world*" (that is the circle of careless and ungodly people around us) ; the world will feel condemned by this example of Christian faith and life, and is sure to take some revenge by ridicule, or slander, or reproach. Sceptics and unbelievers, who oppose their dogmas to the plain and honest teaching of the New Testament, will often direct "their arrows, even bitter words," against those who refuse to submit to their instructions. Although bodily persecution is put down, the sincere follower of the faithful and devoted servants of our Lord Jesus Christ must be prepared for some measure of obloquy and contempt ......But oh ! according to the widest interpretation of "*suffering* for the testimony of the truth," can we say that we have ever suffered anything in this holy cause ? Or if unpleasant consequences have sometimes attended our taking a right and faithful course, how can such trials be accounted as anything, when compared with the persecutions which the holy martyrs endured ! It is well that our prayers should rise to the highest standard of Christian virtue, if only to remind us of what we profess to be.

The cross our Master bore for us, for Him we fain would bear ;
But mortal strength to weakness turns, and courage to despair !
Then mercy on our failings, Lord ! our sinking faith renew,
And when Thy sorrows visit us, oh send Thy patience too.

Heber.

THE MARTYR'S HEART.

"Ye shall be witnesses unto Me."—Acts i.

To have the spirit of a martyr is to be true at all costs to the best and highest life that you know. To be a Christian martyr is to be a witness for Christ, and an example of Christian life in the midst of an unchristian and sinful world. Whoever willingly, and with no thought of reward, risks his life to save others; whoever cheerfully suffers loss rather than do a dishonourable action; whoever faces persecution rather than abandon what he knows to be right, he has the martyr's heart. Only be true to your God, be true to your Saviour, be true one to another, be true to the highest that you know, and you, too, shall receive a martyr's crown. Yon shall have the high honour of helping forward by your example the cause of God; you, too, shall be one of Christ's witnesses *.

A PRAYER BY JOHN HUSS, MARTYR, A.D. 1415.

O most Holy and Faithful Saviour, draw our feeble souls after Thee; for unless Thou draw us we cannot follow Thee. Give us a firm and ready spirit; and, because the flesh is weak, let Thy grace prevent, and accompany, and follow us. For without Thee we can do nothing. Grant to us a ready spirit, a fearless heart, a right faith, a firm hope, a perfect charity, that we may with patience suffer and do all for Thy sake. Amen.

---

* Farrar.

YOUTHFUL MARTYRS OF OUR OWN TIME.

I.

DURING a war in India, an English boy was taken captive by an infidel.

"Now," (said the tyrant) "say that you renounce your faith in Christ, or I will compel you by scourging.

The boy refused. He was severely flogged.

"Now," (exclaimed the persecutor) "what is your God able to do for you?"

"*He helps me to bear this patiently,*" was the reply.

The blows fell with greater fury.

"What can your Saviour do for you now?" exclaimed the baffled monster.

"*He helps me to forgive and pray for you,*" replied the dying child.

Again the blows descended.

"What is your Saviour doing for you now?" said the enraged tyrant.

"*He is waiting to receive my soul,*" was the answer. And with these words the martyr breathed his last.

* * * * *

II.

Have you heard of the courage and martyrdom of a Norwegian boy twelve years of age? He lived in Norway. His parents were gone away to America. One day he was walking alone near a river, when he met some idle boys who said to him, "We want you to go and steal some apples in that orchard for us." He replied, "*I will not do so for anybody.*" They said, "We will make you." Again he said, "*I won't do it.*" They said, "If you won't, we will duck you in the river." "*I will not steal,*" he replied.

Then these cruel cowardly boys took hold of him, and dragged him down to the river, and notwithstanding all his cries to spare him, they put him into the river and ducked him. And when they had kept on doing this for some time they said to him, "Will you do it now?" "*No!*" he said. "Then we will conquer you;" and they ducked him in the water again and again. And every time he came up they said, "Will you steal the apples now?" and he said repeatedly, "*No!*" And at last they drowned him.

They did not intend to do it, but they did it. And that boy died a martyr, because he would not do what he knew to be wrong *.

*   *   *   *   *

"SAYING 'YES' TO JESUS."

A boy, who was lying without hope of recovery in a hospital at Bristol, was visited by his father on the evening before his death. "Good night, my dear boy," (said the weeping parent) "I fear we shall not meet again in this world."

A sick man, lying on a bed close by, overheard these parting words; and, soon after, he asked the lad if he had understood what his father meant.

"*Yes*" (replied the dying boy), "*I know I have not long to live. I may die before the morning.*"

"And are you not afraid of death?"

"*No!*" (he answered) "*I am safe and happy. I am not afraid to meet my Saviour.*"

"Oh, that I could say as much as that!" thought the man.

Soon afterwards he asked the boy how he had gained this peace and happiness.

---

* From Vaughan's Sermons to Children.

" There is only one way. You have only to say ' Yes' to Jesus: and then it is all right."

When our Blessed Redeemer was about to suffer and die for our salvation, the voice of our Heavenly Father came to His disciples:—*" This is My beloved Son, in Whom I am well pleased. Hear ye Him."*—St. Matthew xvii. When your hearts answer *" Yes," " Thou, O Christ, art my beloved. Saviour, in Whom I am well pleased,"* then God our Father is well pleased with *you*. You are one of His beloved children in whom He is well pleased. " Being justified by faith you have peace with God, through Jesus Christ our Lord." You surrender yourself, your soul and body, to the power and influence of His Holy Spirit.

From that time you can pray with the Psalmist, " Lord, give Thy strength unto Thy servant. Although often weak, wavering, and unprofitable, I am Thy servant."

It may be His will that you should go through a long training of temptation and trial. One thing is certain, the day and the hour will come when you will be called to leave the world, and give up your soul into the hands of God your Saviour. It may be a death purposely chosen in His service, as, for example, in nursing a brother or sister who is suffering from some contagious disease and by means of it passing to your true home. It may be, you will be called to lay down your lives in doing work beyond your strength. Or it may be, after all, only in falling asleep in Him, like most of His servants in this dying world. In those most solemn moments of your lives, when you kneel before your Creator and Redeemer with these blessed words of self-surrender in your hearts,—*" Here we offer and present unto Thee, O Lord, ourselves, our souls and bodies, to be a reasonable, holy, and living sacrifice unto Thee* * ; " then you are most surely prepared to meet death ; then most surely and thankfully you may look forward to the last unknown hour of trial, and be ready to say with ten thousand times ten thousand who have safely gone before

---

* The Service for the Holy Communion.

you; "*Into Thy hands I commend my spirit: for Thou hast redeemed me* *."

MARTIN LUTHER'S LAST PRAYER.

Oh, my Heavenly Father, Eternal and Merciful God, Thou hast revealed to me Thy Son, our Lord Jesus Christ! I have preached Him, I have confessed Him, I love Him, and I worship Him as my dearest Saviour and Redeemer, Him whom the wicked persecute, accuse, and blaspheme. Into Thy hands I commit my spirit. God of Truth, Thou hast redeemed me.

ARCHBISHOP CRANMER'S PRAYER.

Give me, Lord, Thy grace, that my faith in salvation through Thy blood waver not in me, but be ever firm and constant; that the hope of Thy mercy and life everlasting never decay in me; that love grow not cold in me. Finally, that the weakness of my flesh be not overcome with the fear of death. Grant me, merciful Saviour, that when death hath shut up the eyes of my body, the eyes of my soul may still behold and look upon Thee; that when death hath taken away the use of my tongue and speech, my heart may still cry and say unto Thee, O Lord, into Thy hands I give and commit my soul. Lord Jesus, receive my soul unto Thee. Amen.

" Into Thy hands I commend my spirit."—Psalm xxxi.

"Father in heaven! be Thou my friend; on Thee may rest mine eye—
When at the midnight hour of death a lonely man I lie;
Then whisper in my closing ear, grown deaf to all but Thee,
Alone on His forsaken cross that JESUS died for me!
So when all human help is past, all earthly pleasures flown,
It will not be a bitter thing to die,—to die alone."

---

* Psalm xxxi.   Acts vii. 59.

PERSECUTION.

A LETTER TO THE YOUNG.

"Blessed are they that are persecuted for righteousness' sake, for theirs is the kingdom of heaven."

"Blessed are ye, when men shall revile you, and persecute you, and say all manner of evil against you falsely, for My sake; rejoice and be exceeding glad: for great is your reward in heaven."— St. Matthew v.

"He that overcometh, the same shall be clothed in white raiment; and I will not blot out his name out of the Book of Life, but I will confess his name before My Father, and before His angels."— Rev. iii.

TO THE YOUNGER FRIENDS, SOLDIERS, AND SERVANTS OF OUR LORD AND SAVIOUR, JESUS CHRIST.

DEAR YOUNG FRIENDS,

You remember that it is written among the parting words of our Blessed Saviour to His chosen Apostles, "*Ye shall receive power, after that the Holy Ghost is come upon you, and ye shall be witnesses unto Me.*" (Acts i.) They were called to be *martyrs* * or *witnesses*, in life and in death, to the truth and power of Christ and His gospel.

You, my dear young friends, may never be compelled to endure much suffering or persecution for the Lord's sake. We live in happier days. But you are called to be *witnesses* for your Master and only Saviour, not by

---

* The word *martyr* means a *witness*,—one who gives true testimony in a great cause. A *Christian* martyr is one who gives his testimony by words and deeds to the great truths, facts, and principles of the Christian religion, and who is prepared (if need be) to seal his testimony by suffering and dying for his Saviour's sake.

dying a martyr's death, but by living a Christian life. You will always find some good work to do, and something hard to bear *for His sake.*

You are called not only to be true witnesses and faithful servants, but also true-hearted *soldiers* of our Lord Jesus Christ. From the Day of Pentecost until now, a great battle has been fought. It will last to the second coming of our Lord. It is a continued warfare between God and Satan,—between the Holy Spirit and the Evil One. It is the good fight of faith against unbelief. It is the warfare of holiness against sin. Thanks be to God who giveth us the victory through our Lord Jesus Christ. In this warfare and victory you are called to take your part.

Our Lord Jesus Christ, the Captain of our salvation, has many good and faithful soldiers in His army. But he wants millions more. He wants *your help.* He calls you to shine as lights in a dark world, and, by the silent influence of a blameless life, to adorn the gospel of God our Saviour. God is able to fight His own battles, to defend the faith of His Church, and to maintain His own cause, without our aid. But it is His will, and it is for His glory, that His work should be done and His battles fought by the beloved and chosen followers of His dear Son.

Are you, my dear young friend, one of these? What was the watchword of one of the bravest of our English heroes? "*England expects everyone to do his duty.*"

Your Saviour expects every one of you to take your place in the army of the King of kings, and to do your duty as His faithful soldier and servant unto your life's end. Your name is written in the Book of life. Whenever you kneel in prayer, whenever you enter a Christian sanctuary, and join in the Hymns and Prayers of the Church, you acknowledge Christ to be your Saviour and your King. By every act and sign of Christian faith and worship you profess to be a true Christian,—one of the faithful and true-hearted servants of our God *.

---

* *Sentenced to death!* It is this which makes the sin of *child-murder* so grievous and damnable in the sight of Heaven. Parents

If you love our Lord Jesus Christ in sincerity, you will often pray for wisdom and understanding to *know* His will, and for a faithful and loving heart to *do* it :— " Lord, teach me to do Thy will."

Do not ask, How *much* am I doing for Him ? but *How* am I doing it ? with what motives ? in what spirit ? In the day of judgment all that will remain of a life full of outward activity and labour will be perhaps those *little* every day acts of patience and self-denial, those words of loving-kindness, which will be rewarded openly by our Father who seeth in secret the thoughts and intentions of every heart (St. Matt. vi. 4, and x. 42). For His sake you will abhor and avoid whatever is likely to lead you or your neighbour into sin. If you are tempted, it will require your whole strength, with the help of God, to keep yourselves pure in thought, word, and deed. Christ has faithful soldiers and servants in every street, in every school, in many a crowded dwelling. In these days of sharp dealing, do you stand up for honesty, refusing to defraud or deceive your neighbours by any thievish tricks of trade ? Do you refuse to listen to the hasty babble of the busy mocker,—the profane parody of the half-witty jester,—the spoken impurities and inuendoes of the unclean mind ? Do you persevere in going to your Sunday School, or your Bible Class, in the face of ridicule and scorn ? Are you found constantly in the House of Prayer, and often at the Supper of our Lord ? Do you continue to kneel in morning and evening prayer, like Daniel in Babylon, notwithstanding much weariness and many discouragements ? Do you continue in all this, not to please yourselves or your friends, but because you love and honour God ?

In all this you are a true and faithful witness for the

---

who, by their neglect and carelessness cause the death of their young and feeble children are guilty of depriving the Lord Jesus of some of those who, if their lives had been spared, would have been numbered among His most faithful servants. They rob GOD of *the honour and glory* of leading those martyred children safely through a lifetime of temptation to His heavenly Kingdom. It is good to be removed from this sinful world in childhood. It is better to *live to the glory of God* on earth, and to win a faithful servant's crown.

truth of God's promises. You are confessing Christ before men. You are encouraging friends and neighbours to live unto the Lord. You are cheering the hearts of his ministers 'and all who help them in their blessed work. You shine as lights in a dark world, and add more brightness to the Redeemer's crown. And while you follow your Divine Master you. are glorifying Him on the earth, and finishing the work He has given .you to do.

Every morning, before you go forth to the labours and trials of the day, let your will be strengthened by meditation : let your heart be fixed where true joys are to be found. Pray always for the Holy Spirit *."

> For every virtue we possess,
> And every conflict won,
> And every thought of holiness,
> Are His alone.

PERSECUTION. The servant of Christ is often tried by petty and vexatious persecutions. A jeering word from some old companion ; discouragements from one who ought to help you on ; coldness from those who ought to shew you kindness ; false accusations brought against you, and wrong motives laid to your. charge : all this is hard to bear. Our poor feeble hearts quail before the scorn of man. But Jesus has borne it before us. The apostles and martyrs passed through far hotter trials than yours. And their God will strengthen you and carry you through unhurt.

It is said of John Huss, the Bohemian martyr, that when he was brought out to be burnt, they put on his head a paper crown with painted devils on it. On seeing it he said, " My Lord Jesus Christ, for my sake, wore a crown of thorns ; why should not I, for His sake, wear this light crown ? Truly I will do it, and that willingly." When it was set upon his head, some who stood by said, " Now we commit thy soul to the devil !" " But I,"

---

* O God, forasmuch as without Thee we are not able to please Thee, mercifully grant that Thy Holy Spirit may this day direct and rule my heart, through Jesus Christ our Lord. Amen.

said Huss, lifting up his eyes towards heaven, "do commit my spirit into Thy hands, O Lord Jesus Christ."

And how do *you* feel, if you are reproached, scorned, and denied for Jesus' sake? Oh! try and feel as the disciples felt when they rejoiced that they were counted worthy to suffer shame for His name! (Acts v.) In the hour of trial, look up for strength, saying, "Lord Jesus, help me to bear this, for Thy sake." Strength will be given you: and you will feel it an honour to suffer for your Master's sake.

Be very careful not to lose your temper when spoken against. Let your daily life be your best defence. Think of your Lord, Who, when He was reviled, reviled not again, but committed Himself to Him that judgeth righteously. (1 Peter ii.) The time will come, when those who have treated you scornfully will see their error. Aye, they see it already; but the Evil One urges them on. In a short time your Christian conduct may win over your very persecutors. And, if you repay harsh words and rough treatment with kindness and love, you will be glorifying God and smoothing your own path.

Let me add a word about those persecutions which some *bring upon themselves* by their own inconsistencies and unguarded conduct. We should never forget that it is only to those who are persecuted *for righteousness' sake* that a blessing is promised. (Matthew v.) If therefore we are smarting from unkind treatment, will it not be well to ask whether we may not have brought this evil upon ourselves? There may have been something in our conduct, or our manner of speaking, which has almost *invited* persecution. For instance, we may be a little self-conceited or censorious in our language; we may carry ourselves in an overbearing manner, like the Pharisee in the parable (Luke xviii.) We may have zeal without discretion. Surely we shall do well to take our daily conduct seriously to task, in order to discover and avoid whatever may be causing needless offence.

The charge of being *singular* and too *precise* will probably be brought against you by a mocking world. A true soldier of Christ, in obeying his King's commands, must expect to be ridiculed by those who sit in the seat of the scornful. (Psalm i.) You may be called "over-strict," "puritanical," "goody," &c., &c. St. Paul fore-warned us of the appearance of these "despisers of those that are good" in the last days (See 2 Tim. iii.) You will take the opinions of the mocker, and the sayings of the scoffer, for what they are worth. To your Master in Heaven you stand or fall : and He is able to make you stand (Romans xiv.) The true soldier of the Cross must needs be different from other men in many instances. Avoid singularity as far as possible in manners and conduct. But in *important* matters, where a principle is at stake, there must be a coming out and being separate (2 Cor. vi.) There are certain practices which are positively hurtful to the soul, and hateful to God. These you must carefully avoid if you would be a candidate for Heaven. You must resolutely, and at once, set your face against them.

And here let me consider a question which often perplexes a beginner in the Christian life, "What ought I to give up ? Is it right to go here or there—to do this or that ? The best rules are these :—

1. Ask God to direct you, and to guide your judgment, so that you may see clearly what is the right course. "Lord, what wilt Thou have me to do ? Make Thy will known. Make Thy way plain *."
2. Consult your Bible.
3. Take counsel from Christian Pastors and friends. *God speaks by them.*
4. Go nowhere where you cannot ask God to go with you. Engage in nothing on which you cannot ask His blessing. Avoid late hours. Do nothing which is likely to unfit you afterwards for evening prayer.

---

* O God, Who dost teach the hearts of Thy faithful servants by sending to them the light of Thy Holy Spirit, grant me by the same Spirit to have a right judgment in all things, especially in whatever concerns my peace and safety, through Jesus Christ our Lord. Amen.

5. Whenever you *doubt* about anything being lawful, it is the safer course to avoid it.
6. At the beginning of every day, let your thoughts rise to the life to come. Let your heart be fixed where true joys are to be found.

What is safe for one may be dangerous for another. Our duty is to try and act as we believe God would have us act : and our comfort is, that if we honestly commit our way unto the Lord, He will direct our steps.

DANGEROUS COMPANIONS. It is not only the depraved and profligate that will do you harm, but also the trifling, the idle, and the foolish. But you may find it difficult to get rid of such companions. You must not shake them off roughly. Behave kindly even to those with whom you cannot be intimate : watch for opportunities of doing them good, and try to win them over, by patience and kindness, to the Lord's side. At the same time take a decided course. Cost what it may, you must not let smooth words nor taunts move you from the narrow path.

To hold the place which Christ has given you in His army you will often need the conscientiousness of Joseph, the firmness of Micaiah, the faithfulness of Jeremiah, and the fearless piety of Daniel. "Let your religion be impressive by its consistency, and attractive by its amiableness. A word fitly spoken is valuable : but it is better for persons to *see* the good fruits of your religion. Recommend Christianity in your *life* and *temper* rather than by your tongue."

It will often be found a great relief to a young Christian to let his faith and character be known. This may cost you a struggle. But when once it is known that you are not ashamed of Christ and His service, many difficulties disappear.

" A young naval officer became a truly religious man. For a time he concealed his religious feelings from his brother officers, from the fear of ridicule. Frequently, however, his conscience told him that this was wrong, and that he ought to declare the change in his views.

Happily, a circumstance occurred which delivered him from this difficulty. It was the custom on board his ship to have divine service every Sunday on deck. Now, it had long distressed him, that during the prayers no one knelt. He felt it was wrong, and the sin lay like a weight upon his mind. He determined, on the following Sunday, to do what he believed to be right, though in doing it he should act alone. So, when the prayers began he knelt down. He was now a marked man. He was henceforth looked upon as a "Methodist" and a "saint." He, no doubt, had to take up his cross, and bear something; but his course was now tenfold easier than it was before. He had now come out in his true character as *a Servant of God;* and many of his former difficulties vanished away *.

No boy was more popular at Eton than Coleridge Patteson, afterwards the martyred Bishop of Melanesia. During all his schoolboy life he maintained a noble consistency. At one of the annual dinners given at Slough by the "Eleven" of cricket and the "Eight" of the boat, one of the boys began to sing an objectionable song, and Patteson instantly called out, "If that does not stop, I shall leave the room." This remonstrance being unheeded, he took his departure, followed by some others as brave as himself. Nor was this all: he sent back word that unless an apology was made "he would leave the eleven;" a threat which soon brought the offender to his senses, and made his companions feel that Patteson's consistency was not to be trifled with.

When Captain Hedley Vicars was slain in battle, on the heights of Sebastopol, tears of respect and love were shed over his grave by men who but a few years before would have insulted and mocked him. During six or seven months he had hard work to stand his ground. But the promise failed not :—" The righteous shall hold on his way." "Them that honour Me (saith God) I will honour." (1 Samuel i. 2). Unwavering decision, with

---

* See "The Pathway of Safety," by Bishop Oxenden.

consistency of character and conduct, is the shortest road to that peace and quietness which it is so hard to win among ungodly companions and work-fellows ; it is the surest way to win the respect and confidence even of those who are not religious, but have the good sense to value the fruits of religion.

Ours may not be the popular side. It matters little, if only we are on the side of God and His Truth. Our reward will be that of the saints who suffered and died for God.

*   *   *   *

THE CHRISTIAN FAITH. You are witnesses for our Lord Jesus Christ *in defence of the Christian Religion.*

What is the most powerful evidence for the truth of Christianity? 1. The testimony of the *lives* and deaths of our great and good Christians. 2. The testimony of *our own* life and *our own* experience. Every morning remember that you are going forth to your daily employment as *one of the lights of the world.* (St. Matthew v. Philippians ii. 15.) By the bright example of your every-day life, and especially by your Christian firmness and consistency in times of temptation and trial, *you are helping to keep alive the light of God's truth* in this and other lands. Or you are helping to quench it by weakness and indecision.

But, for this life of a true believer, how great an increase of *faith* is required ! You must have a firm and definite belief, and a fixed rule of daily life. You must believe the truth, the whole truth, and nothing but the truth, about God and your own soul. Nothing less than this has satisfied and sustained the Apostles and Martyrs of Christ ; and nothing but this will satisfy and sustain *you.* Once obtain a real knowledge, aye, one true and glorious glimpse, of *what the Lord Jesus* was to *them* in life and in death, and of *what He is and will be to you,* and you will then, and only then, be able to say, with all His faithful witnesses, "The life which I now live, I live by faith in the Son of God, Who loved me, and gave Himself for me." Your Saviour will take *His rightful place* in your hearts. You will confess Him before men.

You will be ready to join in the Psalmist's prayer, "Incline my heart unto Thy testimonies, and not to covetousness." You will sympathize with his experience when he says, "Mine eyes gush out with water, because men keep not Thy law." You will understand his meaning when he declares that "in keeping of God's commandments there is great reward: and in every time of trial, when you are drawn different ways by conflicting motives, you will 'choose that good part which shall not be taken away' from you."

Who, among the sons and daughters of all nations, have loved God their Saviour most fervently? Who have served Him most faithfully? Who have been most ready to sacrifice themselves, not in vain-glory, or for the praise of men, but *for His sake?* It is written for evermore in the history of nations and families.

We point with confidence to all who have been able to say from the heart, "I believe in God the Father Almighty, Maker of heaven and earth: And in Jesus Christ His only Son our Lord, Who rose again the third day and ascended into heaven; from thence He shall come again, at the end of the world, to judge the living and the dead. And I believe in the Holy Ghost, the Lord and Giver of Life: In the forgiveness of sins; the Resurrection of the body, and the Life Everlasting."

Confidence in the Bible. To live the life, and enjoy the peace and comfort, of a true believer, you must have *sufficient confidence* in the truth and value of the Holy Scriptures as the inspired Word of God. No substitute will ever be found for the Bible. It is the never-failing treasury of strength and comfort to suffering and toiling millions of our fellow-creatures in all pain and sorrow, and in all the fears and agonies of their dying hours. "There is but One Book for me now," said one of the greatest of our novelists and historians, when his end was near *.

There are hasty and vapid writers, who seem to find a diabolical kind of pleasure in raking up old objections to

---

* Sir Walter Scott.

revealed religion, and in weakening and destroying the foundations of the great and precious truths, the true value of which they have never understood. But, surely, no philosopher worthy of the name, no sincere philanthropist, no real Christian, will ever take part with those destructive speculators who weaken or destroy the confidence and the comfort of their weaker brethren in the holy and inspired word of God *.

Never let it trouble you to meet with difficulties in the Holy Scriptures. Be thankful that the most important passages are plain and easy. There are many mysteries which you will never fully comprehend. But the dawn will come, and the shadows will flee away. "*Now* I know in part; but *hereafter* I shall know even as also I am known."

Give up the Bible? Despise the Holy Scriptures? Never. Never while one spark of gratitude remains to the Giver of every good gift. Never while we remember how many millions of suffering, sorrowful, toiling human beings have found comfort and support from its sacred pages, in their most bitter trials and sorrows, and in all the unknown agonies of their dying hours. Give up the Bible? Neglect the devout reading of the Holy Scriptures? Never, while common sense and common gratitude remain. Never, when we know and remember how precious that Book has been to our martyred forefathers, and to all the devoted and faithful servants of our God.

Let it be our heartfelt prayer for all who would rashly destroy our hope in Christ as our Divine Redeemer, for all who weaken or despise the childlike confidence of

---

* The best way to meet the hasty talk of the infidel and the scoffer is to remain *silent*. "Enter not into controversy with persons obstinately perverted in matters of religion : for, instead of converting them by your persuasions to the truth, you will but harden them the more, and endanger yourself. They are to be dealt with in these matters only by persons of great abilities : for a perverted mind and obstinate spirit carries in it a contagion, as infectious as the plague in the body, where their opinions meet with a young and weak opponent."—*Sir Matthew Hale.*

Christ's little ones in their Holy Bible ; "*God forgive them, for they know not what they do*!*"

PRAYER THE REMEDY FOR DOUBTS AND FEARS. Who is not sometimes weak in faith. Who does not mourn over the doubts and perplexities which arise in the heart? Who does not hope and pray for the time when all fears and doubts shall vanish away for ever? The secret difficulties which now trouble you will turn to your profit, if they lead you to pray more earnestly for the light of God's Holy Spirit. Faith is the gift of God. No man can say, "*Jesus is my Lord and Saviour*" but by the Holy Ghost. (1 Cor. xii.) Draw closer to Him in prayer and meditation. Pray for the heart and *the will* to believe the whole counsel of God. You will receive power after the Holy Ghost has come upon you. You will find wondrous things in His word, which you knew not before. A few fervent prayers, renewed day after day, will do more to remove your doubts than all the volumes and arguments which have been written in defence of the truth. We shall need these prayers to the last : "*Lord increase our faith.*" "*Lord, I believe : help Thou mine unbelief.*" "*It is of Thee, O Lord, alone, that we can believe. It is not of ourselves : it is Thy gift. Do Thou, of Thy great mercy, stir our hearts. Quicken us to a stronger and more steadfast faith, that we may yield ourselves to Thee this day and for ever, that in life and in death we may be faithful and true witnesses to Thy power and love.*"

Take your right place *now*, where you hope to be found at last ; not among those to whom the Gospel is foolishness, but with them that are saved, to whom it is the power of God. On the Rock of Ages you will find

---

* Lord Macaulay wrote of a very eminent person who had deeply offended him :—" I did not think it possible for human nature, in an educated and civilized man,—a man, too, of great intellect,—to have become so depraved." We may surely be pardoned if we apply words of almost equal severity to those thoughtless and short-sighted neologians who are teaching our younger friends to despise the Sacred Volume, and to depreciate the testimony and character of Christ and His Apostles.

a happy security, a sure resting-place, amid the fluctu-
ations of "modern thought" and the strife of doubtful
disputations. And in proportion to the quiet confidence
which you enjoy will be the happiness of possessing your
soul in *patience*, and shewing a meek, charitable, and
peaceable spirit towards those who differ from you. In
the honest and prayerful endeavour to fulfil your duties
towards God and man you will learn to depend upon
your ever-present Saviour.

> " All the fitness He requireth,
> Is to feel your need of Him."

You will learn your daily need of His Holy Spirit, and
the daily reading of the Holy Scriptures, which are able
to make you wise unto salvation through faith which is
in Christ Jesus, will be a part of your daily life. As you
grow older, you will experience more certainty and
comfort. Difficulties and doubts will remain. But
those doubts and difficulties will be lost in the brightness
of God's more "exceeding great and precious promises :"
and your path will be "as the shining light which
shineth more and more unto the perfect day."

THE REWARD OF FAITH. "Blessed are they who
have not seen, and yet have believed." (St. John xx.)
"*And yet have believed !*" The Lord Jesus knows the
difference between the unbelief of *a perverse will*, and
the difficulties of *a feeble faith* which *honestly* and *sincerely*
wishes to believe the truth. Happy are they who
earnestly desire to be led by His Holy Spirit, and continue in prayer for more and more of the light and peace
which He gave to all His faithful martyrs. How highly
favoured were those three chosen disciples who conversed
with our Lord upon the holy mountain ! Yet there is
something *more* promised to those whose mortal eyes
have never beheld Him. His Apostles had not the
opportunity of honouring God by so strong a faith as we,
who simply trust His word, and, having not seen, believe,
and love, and rejoice with joy unspeakable and full of
glory, receiving the end of our faith, even the salvation
of our souls. (1 Peter i.) The chosen three beheld the

glory of our Lord on the day of his transfiguration : they saw some of the company of heaven ; heard their celestial discourse. What could they do but believe that Jesus is indeed the Son of God, the Saviour of the world? But *we,* who have not the testimony of our senses, but admit the evidence of Christian *faith,* obtain thereby this testimony, that we *more especially please God.*

Is there not a voice from heaven, which speaks to you, my younger friends, every morning of your lives? "Be thou faithful unto death, and I will give thee a crown of life." Yes : believe it, there is a safe journey and a happy life before you here on earth. There is rest and a crown of eternal joy and glory reserved for you in heaven. This is your inheritance as the servants of Christ, and the children of God. Oh, forfeit it not by your want of sincerity ! Let your faithfulness and sincerity be known and proved by daily watching unto prayer.

Let me conclude with the triumphant words of one of the most faithful of our English martyrs :—

THE CHRISTIAN'S GAIN.

"He shall receive an hundredfold now in this time......and in the world to come eternal life."—Mark x.

"There is none worthy to be counted a Christian, except he can find in his heart, for Christ's sake, if the confession of His truth requires it, to renounce all that he hath and follow Him. And in so doing he gains a hundredfold more in this life, as our Saviour said to Peter, and hereafter is assured of eternal life; Behold, I pray you, what he loses who in this life receives a hundred for one, with assurance of eternal life.

"O happy exchange ! perchance your outward man will say, if I were sure of this great recompense here, I would be glad to forsake all. But where is this "hundredfold in this life" to be found? Yes, truly, for instead of worldly riches which thou dost forsake, which are but temporal, thou hast found the everlasting riches of heaven, which are glory, honour, and praise before God, angels, and men ; and for an earthly habitation, thou hast an eternal mansion with Christ in Heaven; for even now thou art of the city and household of the saints with God, as is verified in the fourth to the Philippians. For worldly peace, which can last but a while, thou dost possess the peace of God which passeth all understanding; and for the loss of a few friends, thou art made a fellow of the innumerable company of heaven, and a perpetual friend of all those that die in the Lord, from the beginning of the world. Is not this more than a hundredfold? Is not the peace of God, which in this world we have through faithful imitation of Christ (which the world cannot take from us) ten thousandfold more than those things which are most highly esteemed in this world without the peace of God *?"

"May God fill all your hearts with His grace, fear, and love, and let you see the advantage and comfort of serving Him; and may His blessing, and presence, and comfort, and direction, and providence, be with you and over you all †."

Believe me to be,

Your faithful friend,

*   *   *

---

* John Philpot, Archdeacon of Winchester, suffered death by burning in Smithfield, A.D. 1555.
† From a Letter by Sir Matthew Hale to his children.

ON THE

COMMEMORATION

OF

DEPARTED FRIENDS.

COMMUNION WITH DEPARTED FRIENDS.

"I KNOW not (indeed who can know ?) whether the spirits of the just are ever permitted to watch over those whom they have loved most tenderly; but if such permission be given—and who can say it is impossible ?—then it must greatly increase their present happiness, if they see you resigned, patient, hopeful, trusting in that Cross which was their refuge in the hour of dread, and that good Providence to Whose care they fervently and faithfully committed you *."

" Let survivors consider this. Let them remember that the surest proof they can give of their affection to the memory of departed friends is to cherish a holy faith and a holy practice ; to be constant in prayer, and inall religious duties ; to subdue evil passions ; to correct bad tempers ; to be honest and just and true in all their ways ; to be faithful in that state of life to which it has pleased God to call them ; and to encourage themselves in perseverance by the consideration that they may possibly be adding to the happiness of the spirits of the just at the very time that, with fear and trembling, yet with faith and patience, they are working out their own salvation, because they know that God is working in them, by His Holy Spirit, to will and to do of His good pleasure †." (Philipians ii.)

If the intermediate state is a condition of progress for happy souls, we may conceive of blessed ministries which departed spirits may fulfil even from their abode in that spirit-world which is the scene of their growth into perfection. A life of special training here may have prepared them for holy duties there ; and we may believe that their graces and virtues, which were developed amid trials and labours in this present life, shall find their full employment where trials and sufferings are unknown.

* Bishop Heber,
† Prebendary James, D.D. (Peterborough).

Holy Scripture permits us to cherish a belief in the enduring sympathy of our departed friends. The faithful departed, who loved us on earth, love us still. Their love may sometimes be permitted to afford us help which we know not. Gentle footsteps may be near us with unseen ministries. Loved faces, cleansed from the dishonours of the grave, may be gazing on us with an immortal sympathy.

We know not if these natural suggestions of love are true; and we thank God for the veil which He has mercifully interposed *." In leaving us in this uncertainty He has saved us from the snare into which we should have fallen, if we were assured of any intercourse, or help, or intercession on the part of the members of the invisible Church. Instead of resting in their love, or trusting in their prayers for us, we look the more steadfastly to the Saviour Who is always with us, and ever liveth to make intercession for us.

Those who are departed in His faith and fear knew whom they believed. It was by the humility and the sincerity of their faith that they were saved from unbelief, and insanity, and despair. They trusted in no false Christ. They obeyed no Phantom King. Their Redeemer and their Lord was the Christ of Bethany and the Mount of Olives, the same Jesus whom St. Paul preached, the only Saviour in whom St. John believed, and Who has been revealed to all who have laboured and suffered for His sake from the Day of Pentecost until now.

> . . . . For there are martyrs now:
> Thousands, unknown to us but known in heaven,
> In many an earthly home *for Him* endure
> Day after day a lifelong martyrdom.
> They spend their years in labour and in prayer,
> In faithful services, in daily strife
> Both with the ill within them and without;
> In self-denial that, by slow degrees
> Wearing the mortal vessel out, at length
> Shall unimprison the immortal light †.

---

* " Sir, in these matters I am so fearful that I dare not speak further, yea, almost none otherwise, than as the Scripture doth, as it were, lead me by the hand."—*Bishop Ridley*.

† See Poems by Rev. J. M. Neale.

Wherefore, with comforted and quickened hearts let us commemorate the holy and the pure who are gone before us into Everlasting Life. The homes where they dwelt are full of painful yet blessed memories. From their earthly dwellings where they toiled, and suffered, and prayed for many a year, they have ascended to be for ever with the Lord. In yonder school, the wise and good have left the testimony of their teaching and example. In that house of prayer they honoured and acknowledged the Saviour Whose they are, and Whom they serve for evermore. Sacred are the homes where they lived, and the altars where they worshipped.

And in spirit they may be with us still. It may be possible, God knows; it may be given them to mark our efforts to glorify God in our appointed duties and callings. Some have thought that they rejoice in our unity; that they mourn when divided counsels separate us, or when a hasty spirit of innovation hinders the work and worship of the Church they loved *.

Let us therefore live *as if* they were still with us in spirit: let us walk worthy of such friends; and let us prepare to enjoy the fulness of communion with them hereafter. Oh, let us bless God for their examples; let us pray for strength to emulate their self-denial, for grace to labour patiently and hopefully in the service of God, even as they laboured, to live as they lived, to die as they died. "And then, when we too are called to our God; when the pilgrimage of life is over; when the heat and burden of the day have been bravely borne; when the watching eyes are closing in death, and the weary head is at rest, may we pass into their blessed company, and with them in hope and bliss await the hour for which the angels are longing, and the Church is praying, the hour when the number of the elect shall be completed, and the kingdoms of the world become the

---

* May we not believe that departed spirits, who are at rest in Paradise, may be permitted, at intervals, to know of the welfare of their friends on earth; when those they love are passing through some great sorrow, with the help of God, or when they gain a new victory over sin and Satan?

kingdom of our Lord Jesus Christ *." "And I heard a great voice out of heaven saying, Behold, the tabernacle of God is with men, and He will dwell with them, and they shall be His people, and God Himself shall be with them, and be their God." (Rev. xxi.)

THANKSGIVING AND COMMEMORATION,

used by the Archbishop of Canterbury and Mrs. Tait, after the death of their children.

" Thus were we called upon to part with these five most blessed little daughters, each of whom had been received in prayer, educated with prayer, and now given up, though with bitter anguish, yet with prayer and thanksgiving.

" Now, constantly, with our daily prayers, we say for them this thanksgiving and commemoration † :—"

Lord, Thou hast let Thy little ones depart in peace.

Into Thy hands, O God, we have commended their spirits, for Thou hast redeemed them, O Lord, Thou God of truth.

Thou hast brought their souls out of prison ; and now they praise Thee.

Thou hast delivered them from the body of this death.

Thou hast said unto their souls, I am Thy salvation.

Thou hast said unto them, To-day shalt thou be with Me in Paradise.

Now they feel the salvation of Jesus ; now they feel the anointing of Christ, even the oil of gladness, wherewith Thou art anointed.

Thou hast guided them through the valley of death. Now they see the goodness of the Lord in the land of the living.

Thou, O Lord, hast commanded their spirits to be received up to Thee in peace.

O Lord, Thou hast bid them come unto Thee.

Lord Jesus, Thou hast received their spirits, and hast opened unto them the gate of everlasting glory.

Thy loving spirit leads them forth into the land of

---

* " The Destiny of the Creature," by Bishop Ellicott.
† Narrative by Mrs. Tait.

righteousness, into Thy holy hill, unto thy heavenly kingdom.

Thou didst send thy angel to meet them, and to carry them into Abraham's bosom.

Thou hast placed them in the habitation of light and peace, of joy and gladness.

Thou hast received them into the arms of Thy mercy, and given them an inheritance with Thy saints in light.

There they reign with Thy elect angels, Thy blessed saints departed, Thy holy prophets and glorious apostles, in all joy, glory, felicity, and blessedness, for ever and ever. Amen.

Glory be to Thee, O Lord, for all Thy servants departed this life in Thy faith, fear, and love. Give us grace, we beseech Thee, so to follow their good examples, that with them we may be partakers of Thy Heavenly Kingdom. Grant this, O Father, for Jesus Christ's sake, our only Mediator and Advocate. Amen.

SHALL WE MEET?

BY H. L. HASTINGS.

Shall we meet beyond the river,
   Where the surges cease to roll?
Where, in all the bright forever,
   Sorrow ne'er shall press the soul?
Shall we meet with those departed,
   Who have bowed beneath death's wave?
Shall we meet the holy myriads,
   Who are ransomed from the grave?

Shall we meet in that blest harbour,
   When our stormy voyage is o'er?
Shall we meet and cast the anchor,
   By the fair celestial shore?
Shall we rest from all our labours
   'Mid the swelling of the tide?
Shall we meet and rest for ever,
   By our blessed Saviour's side?

Shall we meet in realms of glory,
    With the ransomed and the blest?
Shall we meet with all the holy,
    When they enter into rest?
Shall we meet with those whose brightness
    Shall the noonday sun outshine?
Who shall bear the Saviour's likeness
    In its majesty divine?

Shall we meet with many loved ones
    Who were torn from our embrace?
Shall we listen to their voices,
    And behold them face to face?—
All the cherished and the longed for,
    Those whose graves are moist with tears?
Those whose absence made life weary
    Through the dark and tedious years?

Shall we meet with Christ our Saviour,
    When he comes to claim His own?
Shall we know His blessed favour
    With the martyrs near His throne?
Will He bid us share His glory,
    Where no shame shall ever be?
Will he bid us sing His praises,
    On that radiant crystal sea?

Shall we meet the shining angels
    Who have guarded us while here?
Shall we listen to their welcomes,
    And return their words of cheer?
Shall we be their bright companions,
    Far beyond this land of tears?
Shall we share their holy raptures
    Through the lapse of endless years?

Shall we meet, oh! lonely pilgrim,
    When the burden we lay down?
Shall we change our cross of anguish
    For the bright, unfading crown?
Do we love our Lord's appearing?
    Shall we gladly see His face?
Shall it beam with smiles of welcome?
    Shall He bring us endless grace?

Shall we meet, O weary wanderer,
    Say, O will you meet me there,
Meet in glory, not in darkness,
    Meet in joy, and not despair?
When before the throne of judgment
    We shall all together stand,
Will you pray and strive to meet me
    With the blest at Christ's right hand?

THE MEETING PLACE.

"We who have believed do enter into rest."—Heb. iv.

Where the faded flower shall freshen,
  Freshen never more to fade ;
Where the shaded sky shall brighten,
  Brighten never more to shade :
Where no shadow shall bewilder,
  Where life's vain parade is o'er ;
Where the sleep of sin is broken,
  And the dreamer dreams no more :
      Father, we shall meet and rest,
      With the holy and the blest.

Where no friends are ever parted,
  Where no enemy can come,
Where God's servants are as angels,
  In one everlasting home ;
Where the child has found its mother,
  Where the mother finds her child,
Where dear families are gathered,
  That were scattered in the wild :
      Brother, we shall meet and rest,
      With the holy and the blest.

Where the hidden wound is healèd,
  Where the blighted life re-blooms,
Where the smitten heart the freshness
  Of its buoyant youth resumes ;
Where we find the joy of loving,
  As we never loved before,
Loving on, unchilled, unhindered,
  Loving once and evermore :
      Sister, we shall meet and rest,
      With the holy and the blest.

Where no friends are ever parted,
  Where no enemy can come,
Where Thy servants are as angels
  In Thy everlasting home ;
Where our KING is seen in glory,
  Such as earth has never known,
In the day when all the nations
  All Thy love and power shall own,
      Grant us, LORD, eternal rest,
      With the holy and the blest *.

*   *   *   *   *

* See Hymns of Faith and Hope, by H. Bonar, D.D.

Praise the Lord ! for He is glorious,
  Never shall his promise fail ;
God hath made his saints victorious,
  Sin and death shall not prevail.
As the saints in heaven adore Thee,
  We would bow before Thy throne,
As the angels serve before Thee,
  So on earth Thy will be done *.
    Grant us, LORD, eternal rest,
    With the holy and the blest.

PRAYERS.

One or more of the following prayers may be used in moments of difficulty, danger, and temptation.

THOU, O God, seest me.
Lord, help me through this.
Leave me not, neither forsake me, O God of my salvation.
Direct the thoughts of my heart.
Help me to bear this patiently.
Set a watch, O Lord, before my mouth, and keep the door of my lips.
    (See also verses in Psalms xxv., xxvii., and lxxxvi.)

IN PERSECUTION.

THE Lord Jesus grant us His heavenly grace and strength, that we may confess Him in the world among this sinful generation ; that He may confess us at the last day before His Father Who is in heaven, to His glory and our everlasting comfort, joy, and salvation. Amen.

Bishop Ridley.

O LORD Jesus Christ, Saviour of the world, mercifully grant us, we beseech Thee, the full benefit of all those sufferings and sorrows which Thou didst endure for us, that following Thee even unto death, we may be saved for evermore, through Thy merits. Amen.

O God, merciful Father, Who hearest the sighing of a contrite heart, and the desire of such as be sorrowful, mercifully assist our prayers in all our troubles and adversities whensoever they oppress us ; and graciously hear us, that those evils which the devil or man worketh against us may be brought to nought, and by the providence of Thy goodness they may be dispersed ; that we Thy

---

* Kempthorne.

servants, being hurt by no persecutions, may evermore give thanks unto Thee in Thy holy Church; through Jesus Christ our Lord. Amen.

A PRAYER FOR THE YOUNG.

O GOD, Who never failest to help and govern them whom Thou dost bring up in Thy steadfast fear and love, Keep me, I beseech Thee, under the protection of Thy good providence. Strengthen me with the gifts of the Holy Ghost. Enable me to resist temptation. Give me boldness, the resolute mind, the fear of sin, tenderness of conscience, steadfastness, that no persuasion of evil companions, nor ridicule, nor false shame, nor any pleasure which sin promises, may draw me away towards the paths of hell. Grant that, being steadfast in faith, and joyful through hope, I may abide in Thy love, and bring forth the fruits of the same, to Thy praise and glory, and be everlastingly rewarded, for the sake of Thy blessed Son, our Saviour Jesus Christ. Amen.

FOR TRUST IN GOD.

O ALMIGHTY Lord, Who never failest them that trust in Thee, give me grace in all difficulties and distresses to have recourse to Thee, to rest and depend upon Thee. Thou wilt keep him, O Lord, in perfect peace whose mind is stayed on Thee : O let me always rest upon this promise, and never exchange it for the broken reeds of this world. Suffer not my heart to be overcharged with the cares of this life, but grant that, having by honest industry and the use of all lawful means done my part, I may cheerfully commit myself to Thy providence, casting all my care upon Thee, and being anxious for nothing but to be of the number of those whom Thou lovest and carest for with an everlasting love ; seeking first Thy kingdom and the righteousness thereof, may I steadfastly trust in Thee for such a measure of those needful earthly blessings as Thou in Thy wisdom seest to be most expedient for me. Grant this, O Lord, for Jesus Christ's sake. Amen.

FOR PERSEVERANCE.

O ETERNAL and Unchangeable Lord God, Who art the same yesterday, to-day, and for ever, be pleased to communicate some small ray of that excellency, some degree of that stability, to me, thy sinful creature, who am light and inconstant, and turned about with every blast. My understanding is very deceivable ; O establish it in Thy truth, that I may not be led away by the error of the wicked, nor fall from my own steadfastness.

My will also is irresolute and wavering, and doth not cleave steadfastly to Thee. My goodness is but as the morning cloud, and as the early dew it passeth away. O strengthen and confirm me by Thy grace, and whatever good work Thou hast begun in me, be pleased to accomplish and perfect it until the day of Christ. Lord, Thou seest my weakness, and the number and strength of those temptations I have to struggle with ; O leave me not to myself, but in all spiritual combats make me more· than conqueror through Him Who loved me, and gave Himself for me. Let no terrors or flatterers of the world, let no corruptions of my own flesh, ever draw me from my obedience to Thee ; but grant that I may remain steadfast, unmoveable, always abounding in the work of the Lord ; and by patient continuance in well-doing, may seek, and at last, by Thy mercy, obtain glory, and honour, and immortality, and eternal life, through Jesus Christ our Lord. Amen.

A LITTLE LONGER.

"You have need of patience . . . yet a little while."—Heb. x.

A little longer I must bear my sorrow ;
  A little longer bow in grief my head ;
A little longer ; then a bright to-morrow
  Its golden sunlight on my path will shed.

The night of weeping will not last for aye,
  The roseate hues of morn will soon appear ;
The gloom of darkness yield to glorious day,
  And peace and joy succeed to doubt and fear.

O happy hour, long waited for in vain !
  O blissful dawn, speed on thy rapid flight !
Great God, as once of old, so now again,
  With power creative say—"Let there be light."

Light to reveal to me Thy wondrous grace,
  Light to make plain the path to heaven above ;
Light beaming down on me from Thy dear face,
  And shewing me Thy very heart is love *.

---

* G. Washington Moon.